The
WOMEN'S
HAGGADAH

T H E

....

W O M E N ' S

....

HAGGADAH

....

E. M. B R O N E R
with Naomi Nimrod

*Hebrew translations
by Efrat Freiman*

HarperSanFrancisco
A Division of HarperCollins*Publishers*

The Women's Haggadah was conceived by E. M. Broner and Naomi Nimrod and revised thereafter by E. M. Broner.

FIRST EDITION

Library of Congress Cataloging-in-Publication Data
Broner, E. M.
    The women's Haggadah / E.M. Broner with Naomi Nimrod.
      p. cm.
    English and Hebrew.
    ISBN 0-06-061143-X (pbk.) : $10.00
    1. Passover—Prayer-books and devotions—English.
  2. Seder.   3. Women, Jewish—Prayer-books and devotions.
  I. Nimrod, Naomi. II. Haggadah. III. Title.
  BM674.795.B76   1994
  296.4'37'082—dc20   93–21435
                                            CIP

94 95 96 97 98 ❖ HAD 10 9 8 7 6 5 4 3 2 1

This edition is printed on acid-free paper that meets the American National Standards Institute Z39.48 Standard.

F O R

. . . .

those who are wise, contrary, simple,

or do not even know how to question,

may this book be a path.

CONTENTS

....

1

Introduction

9

The Order of the Seder

21

The Women's Haggadah

ACKNOWLEDGMENT

TO MY EDITORS:

....

Kandace Hawkinson, who smoothed the way.
Hilary Vartanian, who found it.
And Jeremy Broner and Aviva Hay for judicious
editorial comment.

. . . .

With women, holiday begins before ceremony, with cleaning, preparation, presentation. If seder is order, that Spring of '75 in Haifa we changed the order.

We three women—a Member of Parliament, a social worker, and I—announced somewhat hubristically that we were holding a "Seder of the North."

But this would be different. The invited men would prepare the meal, serve, and clean. The women would contemplate the traditional Haggadah and write new and relevant prayers.

The American men agreed. My husband, Robert, made a potato kugel. Michael and Davida Cohen drove in from their *moshav*, a cooperative farm, Michael bearing his lemon-stuffed chicken breasts while Davida thought of additions to the Haggadah.

Marcia Freedman, American-born member of the Israeli Knesset, or parliament, came with women's prayers. Nomi Nimrod, social worker, composed a prayer of Miriam driven mad by losing her role as prophet. I wrote the questions of the four daughters instead of the traditional questions of the four sons. Robert and I both sat at the head of the table, each wearing a yarmulke, friends and neighbors surrounding us.

1

Some of the Israelis resisted this role change, certainly our neighbors. The father and son kept to their chairs during the cooking, serving, cleaning up. The woman of the family bawled out an invited singer with, "What will you be when you grow older without a man? Your voice will go and then you'll be nothing." The woman singer stopped singing.

In spite of these interruptions something so startling had happened in that sweet clementine season, something so different emerged from our apartment with its terrazzo floors, that we could actually hear the difference out the window. At the base of Mount Carmel, in the middle or at the top of the mountain, the Jewish citizens of Haifa were reading and singing the Passover service. But our songs had different lyrics.

The next morning Nomi Nimrod phoned. We agreed to meet to talk about delving into sources and writing our own service.

The idea both excited and shocked us.

And so we met daily, despite my teaching and her working schedules, despite the demands of our families.

When we began reading and writing in the study of her late father, a learned cantor, we expected thunder and lightning to come through the roof and crack the walls of the library.

The mother of my collaborator peered anxiously at us from the doorway. What were we doing in her husband's study? Were we desecrating what he had consecrated? His death

2

was so recent that his books were not yet dusty as we pored over them. His widow was sure we were out of our depth, neither of us Judaic scholars.

We did have questions. Since there is no neuter word in Hebrew for God, could there be a designation for holiness that was not solely male?

"Phone Jerusalem," said Nomi. "They feel closer to God there. They'll know."

By "they," Nomi meant the first women rabbinical students who were doing their year abroad at Hebrew Union College.

"What do you call You Know Who?" we asked, once we got the crackly line to Jerusalem.

"Shekhinah," they answered, "She Who Dwells in Our Midst."

"Oh yes!" we said.

The Shekhinah is a Kabbalistic concept, the female aspect of God. She is addressed in prayer, especially during the holidays of Sukkoth and the arrival of the New Moon. The sage Rabbi Yohanan said, "Whoever blesses the New Moon at the proper time is considered as having welcomed the presence of the Shekhinah."

Etymologically, *Shikoon* is neighborhood. *Shekena* is a neighbor. We could nicely use such a neighborly presence as She Who Dwells in Our Midst.

It is said in Israel, "One works in Haifa, plays in Tel Aviv, and prays in Jerusalem." We tried then, in 1975, to work and pray and play in Haifa. We worked at writing a new kind of prayer, using the spine of the traditional holidays, to put women between the covers of the Haggadah, the traditional booklet used at Passover to recount the Exodus. We played with new ideas and we rested, Nomi and I. But at rest we were uncomfortable with the information we were excavating about the extent of the ancient misogyny.

We were uncomfortable with each decision: What to retain and what to restate? How to keep bitterness and anger from overwhelming us? Where to place the traditional stories and yet insert new characters?

I think when we first wrote, "We were slaves unto Pharaoh and the Shekhinah brought us forth," we felt we had invoked the name that would instill strength.

And when we said, "We recline on this night for the unhurried telling of the legacy of Miriam," we had our main character who would encapsulate our journey.

Miriam was the sister of Moses and Aaron. She was the first prophet and she foretold the Exodus; she was the singer at the seashore and the one cast low. After her outcry, "Has the Lord spoken only through Moses?" she was publicly humiliated. Soon thereafter, she died. Nothing more. Only six times was she mentioned in Hebrew scripture—three times in Exodus, named twice only as the sister and once with her song and the title "the prophetess." Then three times in Numbers, her sedition, leprosy, and death. Yet she has haunted our prophets and tellers of legend.

For instance, the prophet Micah speaks with God's voice: "For I brought thee up out of the land of Egypt, / and redeemed thee out of the house of bondage; / and I sent before thee Moses, Aaron, and Miriam." (Micah 6).

And, among the many legends dealing with Miriam, in contrast to the narrow space she occupies in early Scripture, is the one of Miriam and the well. In Miriam's honor, a well of clear, cool water followed the children of Israel through the desert. When Miriam died, the well dried up and disappeared.

We were that well of longing for our history, a well of words pouring forth.

Although Miriam is the parentheses of Exodus, beginning it by peering at the baby Moses, and ending it singing at the shore of the Reed Sea, she is a structure, a construct. What had been omitted from her history was also omitted from our mythic past. It was clearly time for a new Telling.

Nomi and I resolved that we, her modern daughters, would sing Miriam's songs, would reconstruct her journey, and build upon it our own journeys.

It was the Spring of '76 when two groups of women gathered, one on West End Avenue in Manhattan, the other on *Derech HaYam*, Path of the Sea, in Haifa. Both groups had the same text, one in Hebrew, the other in English. Both groups were doing something simple but radical, declaring their right to holiday.

When we think about the first seder in New York in 1976, those of us who were there were altered.

"I feel," says Letty Cottin Pogrebin, "when I think about the seder, a spiritual nucleus for the whole year, a certain kind of transcendence. When there is the seder, it is satisfying and magical."

"I discovered," says Gloria Steinem, "for the first time the purpose of ritual, to make an open space, or a path, for emotions to happen. I thought it was wonderful. Those of us who were motherless became each other's mothers. I have been in my life more refugee than community."

"As far as a community of the seder was concerned," says Letty, "I was happy that smart Jewish feminists were willing to be publicly smart Jewish feminists. There was an organic Judaism increased by a feminist incarnation."

In 1977 *Ms.* magazine, under Letty's careful editing, excerpted *The Women's Haggadah*. And our feminist seder was written up in various newspapers. Gloria Steinem was quoted in a Baltimore paper speaking excitedly of her first spiritual event. Women around the country were shown the *Ms.* version of *The Women's Haggadah* by their daughters. In Toronto, journalist Michele Landsberg cut the excerpted version out of the magazine and used it at her family seder.

Among us, we were forming a community: Letty, Gloria, Phyllis Chesler, and I from the first seder; Bea Kreloff and Lilly Rivlin, as well as our daughters, from the second seder; and, soon, surrogate daughters. Eventually, Bella Abzug, Edith Isaac-Rose, Grace Paley, and Michele Landsberg were to join us. And there were the many guests as well.

We were a tribe. We were a group of women who met once in innocence, achieved a spiritual bonding, and stubbornly continued meeting, planning, and quarreling.

Ms. magazine received hundreds of requests for photocopies of *The Women's Haggadah* over the years. This coincided with the development of the Jewish feminist movement where poets, theologians, and novelists used their Jewish experience as the source. In small enclaves women began meeting at holiday time and inserting themselves into text or composing new text.

The Women's Haggadah, newly revised, enters the season of Passover along with matza, the raising of a wineglass to Miriam, and new names for holiness.

Our referents have altered as biblical research is enhanced by the woman scholar's touch. Grammar has changed with the addition of the third person singular, and lower and upper case "she," and "She," to prayer.

What was omitted is being filled in. What was denigrating is being filtered out.

We thus proceed to a truly inclusive season of exodus.

. . . .

The
ORDER OF
THE SEDER

THE ORDER OF THE SEDER

. . . .

The Passover seder begins with the singing of
the Table of Contents, the Order of the Seder. We,
the women, sing a new order, which I wrote:

THE ORDER

We bless one another
We wash each other's hands.
We dip greens in salt water
And wash pain with tears.

We divide matzot
And hide our past.
We tell Haggadah
And each her own tale.

We bless matzot
And paths in the sand.
We eat maror,
Of the bitter past.

We set the table
For the women's supper.
We find the halved matza
That dropped from our lives.

We end with grace,
With blessing and song.

We greet the night
And the following dawn
In the bosom of friends,
The seder of our own.

At this point there is the *kiddush,* the prayer for wine, and the candle lighting.

Over the years guests have feminized the prayers and I have written new blessings of going into the Passover holiday, or over the Sabbath candles or on coming out of Sabbath.

To whom do we sing?

The Holy One is *Gaol-tanu, Ima-ha-olam,* our Redeemer, Mother of the World.

She is *Ha raham-aima,* Compassionate Giver of Life.

She is *Makor hahaiim,* Source of Life.

She is our neighborly spirit, the Shekhinah.

The women in Jerusalem still know what to call You Know Who.

Our knowledgeable guests alter familiar phraseology. Mikhal Shiff, a cantorial student then at Hebrew Union College, came to us in 1985 to strengthen our voices.

She took this phrase from the traditional prayer:

In every generation,
each man is obliged to see himself
as though he went out of Egypt.

Then Mikhal Shiff sang:

B'chol dor v'dor
Hayava isha lirot

Lirot et atzma ki ilu hi
Ki ilu hi yataz-a mi'mitzrayim

In every generation,
each woman is obliged to see herself
as though she went out from Egypt.

It is still so radical to change the familiar that one's senses are startled.

When the candles are lit, one is mesmerized by the flame, for candles never burn down the same way twice. A thick membrane of melted wax may hang from one. Another tilts dangerously as the flame elongates upward in the slight draft of air.

I would feel the honey of lyrics on my tongue as I sang over the candles.

First we seated ourselves in a circle, close to one another, corded together by memory and melody. I would often wear white, the color of holiday. When I donned my Bucharian yarmulke, the signal was given that time and space were being altered.

We then passed a bowl of water and a towel around the circle as we performed the group ritual of hand-washing. Hitherto, this had been consigned to the "Head of the Household." Here we were both heads and hands.

Candlesticks were distributed among the participants so all could ignite the spirit of holiday.

We light candles, together, as I say:

Together we spread the light
within us is more than light,

there is internal glow,
there is eternal flame.

At our Fifth Seder, 1980, it was *Havdallah,* a Saturday night, the going out of the Sabbath. We removed the white Sabbath cloth. We turned our faces back to the daily.

The twisted *Havdallah* candle was lit, its smoke braiding upward. I sang:

> *Shekhinah,*
> *we sing a new song unto Thee*
> *with soaring melody,*
> *in Miriam's memory,*
> *we sing a new song unto Thee.*

> Hallel *for the Deity,*
> Hallel *for the singer,*
> *with honey on the tongue,*
> *with gift of song,*
> *and beads of words,*
> *we ornament the air for Thee,*
> *we sing a new song unto Thee.*

We prefer to have our women's seder on a night other than Friday so that our friends who guard the Sabbath can attend. We have carelessly or conveniently chosen to forget once in a while and missed valuable women.

Here are two more songs I composed on coming out of holiday.

HAVDALLAH

To mark the difference
to separate, to divide, to set apart.
I will trust and not be afraid

with this congregation of women
and the new beginning together.

and

Blessings on the Shekhinah,
the maker of fire.
Let us be aware
of the division
of light and darkness,
of work and rest,
of self and others,
of holiday and daily.

Let us, as daily women,
as well as women of holy days,
know that there is no holiday
without the preparing for it,
nor is there an ordinary day
unless we make the bed for it.
We are both slaves
and free women.

We pass a spice box around and sniff the odiferous going out of the Sabbath with stick of cinnamon, twig of clove, hard nut of nutmeg.

DRAMA OF THE SEDER
Thereafter, each item in the listed Order of the Seder is noted and has its space.

There are at least three dramatic moments in the seder: lifting aloft the seder plate and pointing out to the assembled the symbolism of its ingredients; opening the door to the prophet; and recovering the *afikoman*, the broken matzo, each of the guests sharing in the eating of it. In the

traditional seder this last act happens after the
seder meal. We, of the Feminist Seder, do not
interrupt for the meal, for the likelihood of our
resuming is slight.

Soon after we begin the seder, we lift the
plate and say:

"This is the seder plate.

"The plate is flat. Woman is flat, like a plate,
flat in the relief of history. Here we give her
dimension in our mythic memory. We do not
merely act as servers but service one another and
make ancient symbols our own."

We name the plate and its objects in the light
of our own gender.

"The *Maror*, often horseradish, representing
bitter herb of our experience, our exclusion.

"The *Haroset*, a mixture of apples-nuts-wine,
representing the mortar of our lives in these new
structures we are attempting to build.

"The *Lamb Shank*, which sets us apart with
special markings, which continues the blood
imagery of the Haggadah and our own bleeding.

"The *Egg*, that which is our rebirth.

"The *Potato* and *Parsley*, for we are earthy,
rooted beings.

"*Salt water* of our tears.

"*Matzot* of our unleavened hearts."

Traditionally, one matza is given special
significance.

That is the *afikoman*, "gift" in Greek, which
is divided in half, and one half hidden. The hidden
matza must be discovered by the children after

the meal so the seder can continue. The adults then bargain with the children to redeem the *afikoman*. Perhaps this custom has to do with completion, with the two parts of the seder connected by the older and younger members. The symbology is lost in antiquity.

In our new tradition we speak of the breaking of the matza as a break, a change, from the old order. We hide the past from ourselves and need to redeem it to create a whole from the broken halves.

In the early days of the Feminist Seder, the daughters who redeemed the *afikoman* requested of us, as their reward, that we care for them, for each other, that we make peace, and that we continue connection.

When Abigail and Robin Pogrebin were about thirteen years old, they set the tone. They wished their mother Letty to have strength and to be what she needed to be in her life.

At the Fifth Seder, the daughters demanded that we pay them off with commitments and blessings, and so we put our hands on their heads and, with full hearts, blessed them. And the group made a commitment to them; we would know them and care about them.

It is the custom for the father of the firstborn son of the priestly tribe of Kohanim to redeem his son from the priestly class. So we buy back our girl children as precious gifts in our lives.

We have said, at our seders, after we've all shared bits of the matza, "Next year in Jerusalem or wherever your Jerusalem lies."

REGENDERING THE HAGGADAH

We have amended the opening words of the traditional Haggadah, "Thou shalt tell thy sons on that day, 'This is on account of what the Lord did for me when I came out of Egypt.'" Instead, we say, "Thou shalt tell thy daughters on that day, 'This is on account of what the Shekhinah did for me when I came out of Egypt,' for we are not sons but descendants of Righteous Women, the Midwives, Shiphra and Puah, Yocheved, the mother of Moses, and Miriam his sister. We were led forth by the *Ruach*, the Spirit, the Shekhinah."

I have sung of the courage of the women in the desert:

> *Slaves were we to Pharaoh*
> *slaves were we to sorrow*
> *but we brought ourselves forth*
> *with our own mighty hand*
> *and left yesterday for tomorrow.*

THE CUPS OF WINE

It is the custom to drink four cups of wine during a seder. Much of the Haggadah is based upon four—the Four Sons, the Four Questions. We use the four *brachot*, blessings, toasts, to mark the phases of our journey. And the toasts have changed along the way from our first to now.

In the version of *The Women's Haggadah* published in *Ms.* magazine in April 1977, the four cups of wine are accompanied by these toasts.

> *I feel the need to be saved.*
> *I wanted to save myself.*
> *From these plagues upon myself,*

I look for the way of self-redemption.
I take the responsibility of becoming a
free woman or a free man.

By 1984, our Ninth Seder, the toasts had
changed:

I begin the journey into my history.
I journey with other women.
To those on the other shore, not able to
risk the plunge.
To the raising high of women who were
laid low.

In the 1992 revision, redemption did not
seem to be the right feeling when women were
under such siege everywhere. Journeying forth
and going back seemed urgent. The toasts were:

We return to Egypt.
We return to the desert.
We drink to the dregs from the cup of
knowledge.
I went to Egypt. I went to the desert.
I learned our history. I am still on my
journey.

Our daughters have a different journey
than we. Our guests have also journeyed from
someplace else. Their markers along the way are
shaped by their lives. But always, our gender
marks the grammar.

THE STORY
The Telling of the Story is the same, yet different,
for there are players upon whom new light is shed

19

in *The Women's Haggadah*. As they are illuminated, so are we. Our studying changes.

What makes the Story different from the traditional readings is the incorporation of self, the insertion of our lives into the tale, to create living history. We speak of our mothers, our fears, hurts, and hopes. And, thereby, we create a new legend.

. . . .

The Women's Haggadah

. . . .

Fill the first cup of wine.

THIS IS THE FIRST CUP OF WINE.

Say, "Here am I, prepared to observe the
mitzvah of the first of the four cups of wine for
the sake of the Shekhinah, Blessed be She."

הִנֵנִי מוּכָנָה וּמְזוּמַנָה לְקַיֵּים מִצְוַות שְׁתִיַּית אַרְבַּע
כּוֹסוֹת יַיִן, לְמַעַן הַשְּׁכִינָה, תִּתְבָּרַךְ שְׁמָהּ.

*Hineni muchana umezumana le'kayem
mitzvat shti'yat arba kosot yayin, lema'an
ha'Shekhinah, titbarach shma.*

This is the first cup of wine.
We drink the first cup, saying, "We return to
Egypt."

אָנוּ חוֹזְרוֹת לְמִצְרַיִם.

Anu hozrot le'mitzrayim.

THE FOUR QUESTIONS OF WOMEN
*Why is this Haggadah different from
traditional Haggadot?
Because this Haggadah deals with the
Exodus of women.*

בַּמֶּה שׁוֹנָה הַגָּדָה זוֹ מֵהַגָּדוֹת מְסוֹרְתִּיּוֹת?
הַגָּדָה זוֹ דָּנָה בִּיצִיאָתָן לַחוֹפְשִׁי שֶׁל נָשִׁים.

Ba'me shona haggadah zo mehaggadot mesortiot?
Haggadah zo dana b'yetzi'atan lachofshi shel
nashim.

Why have our Mothers on this night
been bitter?
Because they did the preparation but
not the ritual. They did the serving but
not the conducting. They read of their
fathers but not of their mothers.

מַדּוּעַ מְרִירוּת אִמּוֹתֵינוּ בְּלַיְלָה הַזֶּה?
שֶׁהֵן טָרְחוּ בַּהֲכָנָה אַךְ לֹא שׁוּתְּפוּ בַּטִּיקְסִיּוּת.
הֵן הִגִּישׁוּ אַךְ לֹא הֵינִחוּ. הֵן קָרְאוּ עַל
אֲבוֹתֵיהֶם אַךְ לֹא עַל אִמּוֹתֵיהֶן.

Madu'a merirot imoteinu be'layla ha'ze?
She'hen tarchu bahachana ach lo shutfu
batixi'yut. Hen hegishu ach lo heenchu.
Hen kar'u al avoteihem ach lo al imoteihen.

Why on this night do we dip twice?
Because of the natural and unnatural
cycles of blood: our monthly bleedings;
the blood spilled by war.

מַדּוּעַ אָנוּ מַטְבִּילוֹת בַּלַּיְלָה הַזֶּה שְׁתֵּי פְּעָמִים?
בַּעֲבוּר הַמַּחְזוֹר הַטִּיבְעִי וְהַבִּלְתִּי טִיבְעִי:
דִּימוּמֵינוּ הַחוֹדְשִׁי; דַּם הַמִּלְחָמוֹת הַנִּשְׁפָּךְ.

*Madu'a anu matbilot be'layla ha'ze shtei
pe'amim? Ba'avur hamachzor hativ'i ve'habilti
tiv'i: Dimume'inu hachodshi; Dam ha'milchamot
hanishpach.*

*Why on this night do we recline?
We recline on this night for the
unhurried telling of the legacy of
Miriam.*

מַדּוּעַ בַּלַּיְלָה הַזֶּה אָנוּ מְסִיבּוֹת?
אָנוּ מְסִיבּוֹת בַּלַּיְלָה הַזֶּה עַל מְנָת לְסַפֵּר
בְּנוֹחוּת אֶת מוֹרֶשֶׁת מִרְיָם.

*Madu'a be'layla ha'ze anu meseyvot?
Anu meseyvot be'layla ha'ze al menat lesaper
benochut et moreshet Miriam.*

We were slaves unto Pharaoh in Egypt. And
the Shekhinah brought us from there with a
mighty hand and outstretched arm. If the Holy One
had not brought out our daughters and sons, our
children's children, we would still have been slaves
to Pharaoh in Egypt. Although if we were all wise,
all sensible, experienced, understanding of the
Torah, it would still be our duty to tell of the

departure from Egypt, and the more one tells of the departure from Egypt, the more she is to be praised.

It is said that four women gathered in Bnai Berak, reclining on cushions and relating the Exodus from Egypt. They are our foremothers: Rachel, Beruriah, Ima Shalom, who was a descendant from the house of Hillel, and her niece, the daughter of Rabbi Gamliel.

Our Mothers spent that Night of Vigil relearning their history until their daughters came to them and said, "Mothers, the time has come to say the morning *shema*."

THE FOUR DAUGHTERS
Through four daughters we shall learn the Torah of Departure. Four daughters and their mothers spent this Night of Vigil seeing themselves as if they went out of Egypt. From Egypt they went out, but not from the house of bondage.

Four questions were asked and four answers were given.

THE SONG OF SEARCHING
Why is this night both bitter and sweet?
The story of women is bitter.
The searching together is sweet.

Why do we dip into the wine of history?
We were led out of Egypt
by the jingle of timbrel,
the echo of song.

What still plagues us in our chronology?
The pestilence of tradition,

the affliction of custom,
the calamity of rabbinic decree.

When shall we lean back comfortably?
We shall not recline
until we find our dignity.

Four daughters arrive, one wise, one wicked, one simple, and one who does not know how to question.

The wise one, what does she say? "Mothers, what did the Shekhinah command of you that you sit here all this night and talk of departures?"

The wicked one, what does she say? "Why are you sitting here all the night, only you women? Women have nothing to say to one another. Women have nothing to learn from one another."

By her saying this, she removes herself from the community of women and isolates herself.

The elderly women tell her, "Because you have broken the chain that links you to our heritage and to the legacy of Miriam, you have no history. You are still in the house of bondage."

The simple one, what does she say? "What is this?" She is referring to the inheritance from Miriam. The older women relate to her the legends about the first prophet.

The one who does not know how to question, for her the others must open the way.

The first mother, Rachel, begins. Rachel, the daughter of a wealthy family, married the shepherd of the household. For this she was disinherited. In spite of her poverty, she sent her husband far away to learn Torah.

Rachel tells of Miriam:

"This legend was told by Rabbi Yehuda bar Zevena. Amram, the father of Miriam, was great in his generation. When he heard Pharaoh proclaim, 'All the sons that are born, ye shall cast into the Nile,' Amram said, 'We are toiling in vain.' Amram divorced his wife, and the men, following his example, also divorced their wives.

"His daughter Miriam said to her father, 'You condemned us more than Pharaoh because he only condemned the males, but you condemned males and females. What Pharaoh decreed was only for this world, but your decree is for this and the next world.

"'Pharaoh is a villain so there is doubt about whether his decree will be fulfilled, but you are a just man so it is sure that your decree will be obeyed.'

"Amram listened to his daughter and took back his wife, Yocheved. All of his followers remarried their wives. The child Miriam and her brother Aaron sang and danced at the ceremony."

Beruriah continues with the narration. Beruriah's wisdom is known far and wide and she is praised in Talmudic literature.

"When Miriam was five her mother was pregnant with Moses. Miriam prophesied, 'My mother is about to bear a son who will save Israel from Egypt.'

"On the day Moses was born, the house was filled with light. Her father, Amram, kissed Miriam on the head and said, 'Your prophecy was fulfilled.'

"Three months later her brother was put into a basket and set floating on the Nile.

"Her father hit her on the head and asked, 'Daughter, now where is your prophecy?'

"That is why it is said in the Hebrew Bible, 'The child's sister took her stand at a distance to see what would happen to him' (Exodus 2:4).

"She was the first of all prophets. Why was she given the name Miriam? *Mar* is bitter, for it was a bitter time. *Mari* is rebellion and *am* is people, for the Jews expressed their bitterness in rebellion."

Ima Shalom, the third mother, received an education befitting the sister of a *nasi*, a leader, and the daughter of Hillel the Great.

Ima Shalom says: "Listen, my daughters, to the story of Miriam. When the time came for Yocheved to give birth, Miriam shared her mother's travails. She predicted Moses, she saved Moses, and she saw to it that he was nursed by his own mother while in the house of Pharaoh. On the night when she and Yocheved put Moses into the water, Miriam, the child, grew up.

"When, years later, it was time for the Exodus, Miriam sang and danced her people to victory. The House of Israel sang a song of freedom to the sound of Miriam's tambourine. The women gathered around Miriam and they

mocked those who cried: 'Leave us alone! Let us
be slaves to the Egyptians. We would rather be
slaves to the Egyptians than die here in the
Wilderness' " (Exodus 14:12–13).

THE SONG IN THE WILDERNESS

We will be slaves to no nation and
    before no man.
We can find our way through the
    wilderness.
We can find our way through thicket
    and stone.
We can find our way under hot desert
    sun to our home.

Ima Shalom continues: "There is a legend
that after the children of Israel crossed the Reed
Sea, they burst into song. When the prophet
Miriam sang, the child on the knee and the
suckling baby saw the Shekhinah. The suckling
baby let go of the breast and started to sing, and
the child on the knee lifted its voice in prayer.
Even the embryos heard singing from the wombs
of their mothers."

THE SONG OF QUESTIONS

Mother, asks the clever daughter,
Who are our mothers?
Who are our ancestors?
What is our history?
Give us our name. Name our genealogy.

Mother, asks the wicked daughter,
If I learn my history, will I not be angry?

Will I not be bitter as Miriam
Who was deprived of her prophecy?

Mother, asks the simple daughter,
If Miriam lies buried in sand,
Why must we dig up those bones?
Why must we remove her from the sun
    and stone
Where she belongs?

The one who knows not how to
    question,
she has no past, she has no present, she
    can have no future
without knowing her mothers,
without knowing her angers,
without knowing her questions.

The daughter of Rabbi Gamliel, who has suffered in her own life, says: "There is anger in our heritage. In the desert Miriam and Aaron asked, 'Is Moses the only one with whom the Lord has spoken? Has He not spoken with us as well?' The Lord passed among them and left Miriam white with leprosy but Aaron unharmed. Miriam was treated like the wicked daughter whose father spat in her face and sent her from the tent for seven days until she was forgiven."

THE LAMENT OF THE PROPHET MIRIAM

Once she danced at the banks of the sea.
Once the women leapt after her.
Then she praised the One on High
and her tambourine rose in the air.

31

And the rain in the wilderness
tasted like coriander,
like almond and honey,
but the taste in her mouth was maror,
bitter as her name.

"You shall be a Kingdom of Priests."
She was not appointed.
"And a land of prophets."
She was not heeded.
"Come up unto the Lord,"
Moses, Aaron, and Seventy Elders.
"Come up unto the Lord,"
Joshua.
"Come up to me into the Mount,
and the Lord spoke unto Moses"
"and the Lord spoke unto Moses"
"and the Lord said unto Moses . . ."
"Moreover, the Lord spoke unto Moses."
"And He gave unto Moses . . ."
"Moreover, the Lord spoke with Moses
and He gave unto Moses
two tables of stone."
"Come up unto the Lord"
"Come up to me unto the Mount
And take Aaron and his sons."

"And the Lord spoke
and Moses . . . the skin of his face
    shone."
"And the Lord spoke with Moses and
    Aaron
and the Lord spoke with Moses

in Mount Sinai."
"And the Lord spoke with Moses
in the wilderness of the Sinai."

"And Miriam and Aaron spoke against
      Moses."
Miriam's face did not shine.
"Behold: Miriam became leprous,
white as snow."

Pale in the wilderness
for the counting of seven days,
shut out from the camp,
tented in dishonor.

Soon, she lay herself down,
the sister of Moses,
the prophet of her people,
she lay down
in a place of no seed, no fig,
no wine, no pomegranate,
no water,
and, parched, Miriam died.

The daughter of Rabbi Gamliel says: "When Miriam died, Moses and Aaron prepared her for burial. It is said that she died with a kiss from the Shekhinah, for the Angel of Death could not take her.

"As Moses brought Joseph's bones out of Egypt, so, Miriam, we will bring your bones out of Kadesh, out of the desert."

The daughters ask, "How did it come about that Miriam was treated so badly?"

"That has to do with the legend of our origins," say the Mothers.

SONG OF OUR SOURCES

We were created together,
the man and the woman,
not one from the other,
not one the helper,
the other the master.
We were created together
for ourselves and each other.

But the rabbis all agree
that woman was created last,
that woman was created least.

Adam was all alone,
jealous of the birds in heaven,
of the reptiles mating on earth,
of the fish in the water,
of the fruit trees in the garden.

The rabbis all agree
that woman was created last,
that woman was created least.

So Adam was given
something a little more
than a bird that sang in heaven,
a creature that crawled on the earth,
a thing that swam in the water.

The rabbis all agree
that woman was created last,
that woman was created least.

She was not made from the head
they said
lest she hold herself too high.
She was not made from the eyes
they said
lest she peer into the sky.

The priests all agree. . . .

She was not made from the ear
for think of the voices she'd hear.
She was not made from the heart
or she would be painfully hurt.

The priests all agree. . . .

She was not made from the hand
or she'd touch everything in the land.
She was not made from the mouth
or soon you would hear her shout.

The ministers all agree. . . .

She was made only from the rib
to do as she was bid.
She was made only from the rib
to do as she was bid.

The ministers all agree. . . .

The men of God agree
that Eve was weak,
that Eve was sinful,
that God on the same day
made Eve and Evil.

The rabbis all agree. . . .

These men, they agree,
but I cannot agree.
My mother was a woman.
My mother was human.
She spoke, heard, touched, felt.
I sing bitterly in this song
that the men of God were wrong.

Originally our foremothers and forefathers
were worshipers of gods and goddesses, and they
dwelt on the other side of the river from time
immemorial until the Shekhinah came. The
Shekhinah took Abraham and Sarah from
the other side of the river and walked them
throughout the land of Canaan. The womb of
Sarah was fertilized by the seed of Abraham and
they bore Isaac. In order to continue the line, the
cousins, Rebecca and Isaac, bore the twins Jacob
and Esau. To Esau and to all of his household—to
his wives, daughters, sons—the Shekhinah gave
Har Seir, even to the wives Ada, the Hittite,
Ahalevama, whose mother was Ana, to Esau's
cousin, Basmot, daughter of his uncle Ishmael,
and to all of the other women who came unto Har
Seir to inherit it.

The first exodus, that of Jacob, Leah,
Rachel, Bilha, Zilpa, and all their household, is
the exodus of one family, and it takes place within
a generation. The second Exodus, from Egypt, is of
the tribes of Israel, descendants of the house of
Sarah and Abraham, whose people dwelled there
over four hundred years.

They went down into Egypt, the descendants of our Mothers: Sarah, Rebecca, Rachel, Leah, Bilha, that bore Naptali, and Zilpa, that bore Asher. They came to Egypt, Jacob and all his descendants with him, his sons and their sons, his daughter and his sons' daughters.

Who of our Mothers went down into Egypt?

Rachel died in childbirth in Beit Lechem. Leah is buried in the cave of Machpelah. Leah's daughter Dina was buried by her brother Simeon in Canaan. Serach, granddaughter of Zilpa and Jacob, is the only woman named among the seventy that went down to Egypt.

The covenant with Israel begins with the promise to Sarah and Abraham that they would not be without offspring, that their daughters and sons would leave Canaan, would sojourn in a land not theirs, would do hard labor for four hundred years. Afterward they would go out with great riches from Egypt and return to Canaan.

V'HE SH'AMDA *The Promise*

And this promise has supported our foremothers, our forefathers, and ourselves, for not only one has risen up against us but in every generation some have arisen against us to annihilate us, but the Holy One saved us from their hands.

V'HE SH'LO AMDA—*The Promise* Not *Kept*

And what is the promise to women? That we have effect on our own lives and the generations that follow us.

In every generation we lost our names and our legacy.

Our role became fertilization of the generations of men.

Our foremothers died and were buried after fulfilling this purpose.

In every generation there have arisen against us those who would destroy us and we have not yet been delivered from their hand.

Lift the second cup.

THIS IS THE SECOND CUP OF WINE.

We drink the second cup, saying: "We return to the desert."

אָנוּ שָׁבוֹת אֶל הַמִּדְבָּר.

Anu shavot el hamidbar.

"Who would rise against our mothers?" asks the Simple Daughter.

"The family and the state," is the answer.

THE STOLEN LEGACY

Beruriah was known for her *midrashim*, commentaries on the law. She guided her husband, Rabbi Meir, in correct interpretation. When Rabbi Meir was upset by the unruly behavior of the people in his section of the city, he prayed for their death: "Let the wicked be no more."

Beruriah said, "In Psalm 104 it says *sins* and not *sinners*. You must pray for mercy toward the people and for the death of the sin."

He did as she suggested.

Beruriah was to have arguments of more serious consequences with her husband later.

Beruriah was infuriated by the attitude of the rabbis toward women. Her conversation with Rabbi Jose Galilee is typical of her sharp wit.

Rabbi Jose Galilee was walking on his way. Beruriah crossed his path. He said to her, "What way should I go to the town of Lod?" She replied, "Galilee—Stupid! Did not our wise men say, 'You should not talk at length with women'? Galilee, you should have asked, 'How to Lod?' "

Beruriah will die before her time and will not conduct more seders. She will die because of jealousy on the part of her husband and the humiliating test he put to her.

Rabbi Meir said to Beruriah, "Women are light-minded." When she objected, her husband warned her that her own end might testify to the truth of his words. Putting her virtue to the test, Rabbi Meir charged one of his students to endeavor to seduce her. After repeated efforts on the student's part, Beruriah yielded. Shame, it is said, drove her to suicide. It is also said that she lies buried on the other side of the cemetery wall.

Which leads us to two questions.

Ima Shalom asks, "Who are the guilty? The woman who yields to temptation, or the man who created the situation in order to test her? Beruriah was dishonored in death, but no dishonor befell her husband or seducer."

The niece of Ima Shalom asks, "And why would such an unlikely story of a virtuous and learned woman be told?

"Because women's learning is anathema. If women read books, soon they will write books. And the heroes and plots will change. If women read Torah, they will write the unsung songs and name the nameless women."

Ima Shalom says, "I learned in the house of the father of my father and was called upon for advice in the house of my husband, Rabbi Eliezer ben Hyrcannus. And yet it was he who said to our son, 'It is better to burn the words of the Torah than to give them to women.'"

Rachel is the daughter of Kalba Shavuah, a wealthy man. While living in her father's house she noticed a modest but good shepherd. Rachel proposed marriage to this shepherd on the condition that he go to the House of Learning to study Torah. When Rachel's father learned of this unsuitable match, he disinherited his strong-willed daughter and threw her out of the house.

Akiva and Rachel moved into a hut and slept on straw. Each morning Akiva would remove blades of straw from his bride's hair. Rachel reminded Akiva of his promise to study in the *Beit Midrash* where she, a woman, would not be allowed. Akiva kept his word and left his wife. Rachel cut her hair and sold the braids to send him money for his studies.

There are stories that Akiva studied for twelve years. Some say it was for twice that, and another legend says that it was for forty years. Rachel continued to live poorly.

When Akiva returned as a great man with twelve thousand students attending him, Rachel, a ragged old woman, approached. His students shoved her away. Akiva then recognized his wife and said to his students, "Do not prevent her from coming to me, for what is mine and yours is hers."

The simple daughter asks, "Is there a husband who sends his wife to study for forty years, twenty-four, or even for twelve, and lives in poverty to maintain her?"

The mothers answer, "Such has not been the custom."

The niece of Ima Shalom, daughter of Rabbi Gamliel, she has no given name: "My father thought I was clever. He respected the answers I gave to an unbeliever.

"When I married and came to him twice for his blessings, this is what he said: 'Let it be that you should not return here.' When I bore a male son, he said to me, 'Let it be that you should never cease from crying, Alas!'

"When I told him, 'Two times happiness came to me and each time you cursed me,' he replied, 'Both curses are blessings. Because I want you to have peace in your home, you should not return here. Because I want your son to live, Alas! shall not cease from utterance from your lips. Alas that my son did not eat! Alas that my son did not drink! Alas that my son did not go to the synagogue.'

"My father no longer remembers me or my learning."

SONG OF THE MOTHERS

Years ago in Bnai Berak
four women learned this saying:
"Because of Just Women
Israel is redeemed from Egypt."

Shiphrah, Puah, brave women,
midwifed a nation
by disobeying Pharaoh.
The Jewish children
were born in rebellion.

But not in the sources
were Just Women rewarded.
Miriam died in obscurity.

Four women on the Night of Vigil
learn of the anger of women.
Though her knowledge of Torah be
    great,
the story of Beruriah is a lesson
that one can be expelled again
for eating of the Tree of Knowledge.

Ima Shalom, from the House of Hillel,
guided her husband Eliezer to wisdom.
Instead of praise, he heaped scorn:
"If Torah be given a woman,
better let it be burned."

Rachel, a reader of Torah,
was disinherited
for choosing knowledge and love.
In poverty with her shepherd she slept,
straw and hay in her hair and bed.

Because she could not learn,
she sent him to learn in her stead
and he studied for forty years,
while she slept on a hard pallet
and chewed hard crusts of bread.

The daughter of Rabbi Gamliel
went the natural course of women
but her father's blessings were curses.
She cried a heaving last, Alas!
In which all the bitterness
of learned women
was expressed.

Lift the third cup.

THIS IS THE THIRD CUP OF WINE.

We drink the third cup, saying, "I drink to the dregs the cup of knowledge."

אֲנִי שׁוֹתָה מִכּוֹס הַיֵּדַע עַד תּוֹם.

Ani shota mekos ha'yeda ad tom.

The Simple Daughter asks the Mothers, "Is there more to be learned?"

"We have to learn of our plagues," says Ima Shalom.

"And of what suffices," says Beruriah.

"And for whom to open the door," says Rachel.

THE PLAGUES OF WOMEN

1. BLOOD
    The bleeding and bearing cycle of the
        female
    is considered unclean by the male.
    She will be killed,
    her blood spilled
    if holy places, priests, and men
    are approached by bleeding women.
    And so woman is forcibly removed
    from power and rule because of blood.

דָּם.
מַחְזוֹרִיּוּת הַדִּימוּם וְהַלֵּידָה
שֶׁל הַנְּקֵבָה
נֶחְשֶׁבֶת לְטֻמְאָה עַ״י הַזָּכָר.
הִיא תֵּהָרֵג,
דָּמָהּ יוּגַר
אִם בְּמָקוֹם טָהוֹר, לַכֹּהֵן אוֹ לְגֶבֶר
תִּפְנֶה אִשָּׁה מְדַמֶּמֶת.
אָז הָאִשָּׁה בְּכֹחַ תּוּרְחָק
מִשִּׁלְטוֹן וְעוֹצְמָה בַּעֲבוּר דָּמָהּ.

DAM
Machzoriut hadimum ve'haleyda
Shel haneke'va
Nech'shevet letme'a al-yedey hazachar.
He tehareg
Dama yuggar
Im bemakkom tahor, lecohen o legever
Tifne isha medamemet.
Az ha'isha beckoach turchack
Meshilton ve'otsma ba'avur damah.

The Tribal Council of Men Did Not Listen to
the Voices of Women.

2. THE FROG: FALSE SELF-IMAGE
A constant froggy smile,
fear of the frown,
the raised voice or hand,

she hops into the house,
to the bedchambers,
falls into pots, ovens,
the kneading trough.
She has squatted so long,
she has no size.

הַצְפַרְדֵּעַ: דִּימּוּי עַצְמִי שִׁקְרִי.
חִיּוּךְ צְפַרְדֵּעִי קָבוּעַ,
פַּחַד מִמַּבָּט זוֹעֵף,
הַיָּד וְהַקּוֹל מוּרָמִים,
וְהִיא מְקַפֶּצֶת אֶל בֵּיתָהּ,
לְחֲדַר הַמִּטּוֹת,
לְתוֹכְכֵי סִירִים, כִּירַיִם, מַלּוֹשׁ.
וְתוֹסִיף לִכְרוֹעַ שָׁם,
עַד שֶׁאִיבְּדָה צַלְמָהּ וּדְמוּתָהּ.

HATSFARDE'A: DIMUI ATSMI SHIKRI
Chi'yuch tsfarde'i kavu'a,
Pachad memabat zo'eff,
Hayad ve'hakkol muramim,
Ve'hi mekapetset el beita,
Le'chadar hamitot,
Letochechey sirim, kiraim, malosh.
Vatosif lichro'a sham,
Ad she'ibda tsalma udmuta.

3. LICE: DISSATISFIED
*She scratches her life
like a lice-filled head.*

כִּנִּים: חֲסָרַת סִיפּוּק.
הִיא מְגָרֶדֶת חַיֶּיהָ
כְּרֹאשׁ נוֹשֵׂא כִּנָּה.

KINNIM: CHASSRAT SIPUK
He megaredet cha'yeha
Kerosh nosse kina.

4. THE GNAT: UNKNOWN
   She fills the eyes with dark spots,
   the ears with buzzing dust.
   Yet, though she is a multitude,
   she is invisible,
   though she is a pestilence,
   unnameable.

שַׁפִּירִית: אַלְמוֹנִית.
הִיא מְכַסָּה עֵינַיִם בִּנְקוּדוֹת כֵּהוֹת,
אוֹזְנַיִם בְּאָבָק מְזַמְזֵם.
וְעַל אַף רִיבּוּיֶיהָ,
הִיא בִּלְתִּי נִרְאֵית,
עַל אַף אַרְסָה,
בַּת בְּלִי שֵׁם.

SHAFIRIT: ALMONIT
He mechasa einaim binkudot kehot,
Oznaim be'avak mezamzem.
Ve'al af ribuya,
He bilti nir'eit,
Al af erssa,
Bat bli shem.

5. NOXIOUS BEASTS

Those who beat her,
ostracize her,
brutalize, make vermin of her,
then fertilize her.

עָרוֹב.
אֵלֶּה הַמַּכִּים אוֹתָה,
מְנַדִּים אוֹתָה,
מִתְאַכְזְרִים אֵלֶיהָ, הוֹפְכִים אוֹתָה לְרֶמֶשׂ,
וְאָז מַפְרִים אוֹתָה.

ARROV
Elle hamakim ota,
Menadim ota,
Mit'achzerim elei'ha, hofchim ota leremes,
Ve'az mafrim ota.

6. BOILS: JEALOUSY

It is recognized in Numbers
that man will be jealous of woman.
There is a grain offering
he comes bearing.
The priest becomes his tool
and issues a priestly rule
that woman must prove she is sinless
but man is always guiltless.
Before the whole community
man is given authority over woman's
    body
and the issue of her womb.

But for woman's feelings
there is neither hearing nor room.

שְׁחִין: קִנְאָה.

מַכִּירִים בְּסֵפֶר בְּמִדְבַּר

שֶׁגֶּבֶר יְקַנֵּא לָאִישָׁה.

עַל כֵּן יֵשׁ קוֹרְבַּן מִנְחָה

שֶׁהוּא מַעֲלֶה לְעוֹלָה.

הַכֹּהֵן מְשַׁמֵּשׁ כְּלִי בְּיָדָיו

וְגוֹזֵר חוֹק קוֹדֶשׁ,

שֶׁעַל הָאִישָׁה לְהוֹכִיחַ חֲפוּתָה

אַךְ הַגֶּבֶר תָּמִיד חַף מֵאַשְׁמָה.

לִפְנֵי קָהָל וְעֵדָה,

נִיתְּנָה לַגֶּבֶר הַסַּמְכוּת,

עַל גּוּף הָאִישָׁה,

וְתוֹצַר רַחְמָהּ.

אַךְ לִרְגָשׁוֹת הָאִישָׁה

אֵין אוֹזֶן קַשֶׁבֶת וְאֵין מוֹצָא.

SH'CHIN: KINN'A
Meckirim be'sefer Bamidbar
She'gever yekane la'isha.
Al ken yesh korban mincha
She'hu ma'ale leola.
Hakohen meshamesh kli be'yadav
Ve'gozer chock kodesh,
She'al ha'isha lehochi'ach chafuta
Ach hagever tamid chaf me'ashma.
Lifney kahal ve'eda,
Nit'na lagever ha'samchut,

Al guf ha'isha,
Ve'totsar rachma.
Ach le'rigshot ha'isha
Ein ozen kashevet ve'ein mot'sa.

**And the Tribal Council Hardened Its Heart
Against Women.**

7. MURRAIN: WOMAN AS SINFUL

Solomon the Ruler said,
"The wiles of women
are more bitter than death.
Her heart is a trap to catch you.
Her arms are fetters
to make man a sinner.
Only by grace of God
can we ever escape her."

דָּבָר: אִישָׁה כִּמְלֵאַת חֵטְא.
אָמַר שְׁלֹמֹה הַמֶּלֶךְ,
"תַּכְכֵי הָאִישָׁה
מָרִים כַּמָּוֶת.
לְבָבָה מַלְכּוֹדֵת לְתוֹפְסֵךְ
זְרוֹעוֹתֶיהָ כְּמוֹסָרוֹת
לְהַבִיא גֶבֶר לִידֵי חֵטְא.
רַק בְּרַחְמֵי הָאֱלוֹהִים
נוּכַל לְהִימַלֵט מִפָּנֶיהָ."

DEVER: ISHA KI'MLE'AT CHET
Amar Shlomo ha'melech,

"Tochechey ha'isha
Marim ka'mavet.
Levava malkodet letofsecha
Zro'otei'ha kemosarot
Le'havi gever li'ydei chet.
Rak berachmei ha'elohim
Nuchal le'himalet mipaneya."

8. LOCUSTS: LEGAL DISCRIMINATION

The generations are figured
from father to son
and thus woman
depends upon man
for he is her legal guardian.
She can keep no obligation,
promise, or vow
that man cannot disallow.
Because she was by the serpent beguiled
she can never be legally more than a
child.

אַרְבֶּה: אַפְלָיָיה חוּקִית.
הַדּוֹרוֹת מְחוּשָׁבִים
מֵאָב לְבֵן
וְעַל כֵּן אִשָׁה
תְּלוּיָה בַּגֶּבֶר
שֶׁהוּא מְגִנָה הַחוּקִי.
הִיא לֹא יְכוֹלָה לְקַיֵּים הִתְחַיְיבוּת,
הַבְטָחָה אוֹ נֶדֶר
שֶׁאוֹתָן הַגֶּבֶר לֹא יַתִּיר.

וּמִכֵּיוָן שֶׁעַל יְדֵי הַנָּחָשׁ פּוּתְּתָה,
לְעוֹלָם לֹא יִהְיֶה מַעֲמָדָהּ
יוֹתֵר מֵאֲשֶׁר כְּשֶׁל יַלְדָּה.

ARBE: AFLA'YA CHUKIT
Ha'dorot mechushavim
Me'av leben
Ve'al ken isha
Tlu'ya begever
She'hu megayna ha'chuki.
He lo yechola leka'yem hitcha'yevut,
Havtacha o neder
She'otan hagever lo yatir.
U'micheyvan she'al yedey hanachash puteta,
Le'olam lo yihi'ye ma'amada
Yoter me'asher keshel yalda.

9. DARKNESS
It became pitch-dark
in the history of women.
They could not see one another.
And none stirred from where she sat.
All lights of learning were dimmed
and the doors of the House of Study
*   were locked.*
The woman could not read.
The woman could not write,
could not take part in her community,
could not participate
in writing her own history.

חוֹשֶׁךְ.
וַיְהִי חוֹשֶׁךְ וַעֲלָטָה
בְּדִבְרֵי יְמֵי הַנָּשִׁים.
וְלֹא תוּכַלְנָה לִרְאוֹת אִשָּׁה אֶת רְעוּתָה.
אַף אַחַת לֹא מָשָׁה מִמְּקוֹם שִׁבְתָּה.
כָּל אוֹרוֹת הַלִּימוּד הוּעֲמוּ
וּדְלָתוֹת בָּתֵּי הַמִּדְרָשׁ נִנְעָלוּ.
הָאִשָּׁה לֹא יָכְלָה קְרוֹא,
הָאִשָּׁה לֹא יָכְלָה כְּתוֹב,
לֹא יָכְלָה לְהִשְׁתַּתֵּף בִּקְהִילָתָה,
לֹא יָכְלָה לְהִשְׁתַּתֵּף
בִּכְתִיבַת דִּבְרֵי יְמֵי חַיֶּיהָ.

CHOSHECH
Va'yehi choshech va'alata
Be'divrei yemei ha'nashim.
Velo tuchalna lir'ot isha et re'uta.
Af achat lo masha mimkom shivta.
Kol orot halimud hu'amu
U'dlatot batei hamidrash nin'alu.
Ha'isha lo yachla kro.
Ha'isha lo yachla chtov,
Lo yachla le'hishtatef bik'hilata,
Lo yachla le'hishtatef
Bi'chtivat divrei yemei cha'yeha.

And the Tribal Council Abandoned the
Women.

10. SLAYING OF THE SPIRIT

It happened that first midnight
when he passed over her
and she bowed her head and worshiped.
With all women it was thus,
from the highborn to the lowly,
they became captive spirits.
And no one heard them cry,
yet, in each house, had the woman
expired.

שְׁחִיטַת הַנְּשָׁמָה.
זֶה קָרָה בַּחֲצוֹת הַלַּיִל הָרִאשׁוֹן
כַּאֲשֶׁר הוּא גָּהַר מֵעָלֶיהָ
וַתֵּרֶכֶן הָאִשָּׁה אֶת רֹאשָׁה וַתִּתְפַּלַּל.
וּלְכֹל הַנָּשִׁים כָּךְ הָיָה,
מֵרָמַת הַמַּעֲלָה וְעַד הַשְּׁפֵלָה,
הֵן הָפְכוּ לִנְשָׁמוֹת כְּלוּאוֹת.
וְאַף לֹא אֶחָד שָׁמַע אֶת זַעֲקָתָן,
וְעַל אַף זֹאת, בְּכֹל בַּיִת, הָיְיתָה
אִשָּׁה שֶׁגָּוְועָה.

SH'CHITAT HANESHAMA
Ze kara bechatsot hala'il harishon
Ka'asher hu gahar me'alei'ha
Va'tarken ha'isha et rosha va'titpalal.
U'lechol hanashim kach haya,
Mi'ramat hama'ala ve'ad ha'shfela,
Hen hafchu linshamot klu'ot.

Ve'af lo echad shama et za'akatan,
Ve'al af zot, be'chol bait, ha'yita
Isha she'gav'a.

AND THE TRIBAL COUNCIL NEVER LET THE
HEBREW WOMEN GO OUT OF BONDAGE.

"But what is *dayenu?* What is sufficient for
us?" asks the Wise Daughter.

DAYENU

If Eve had been created in the image of
   God
and not as helper to Adam,
it would have sufficed.
Dayenu.

אִילוּ נוֹצְרָה חַוָּה בְּצֶלֶם אֱלוֹהִים
וְלֹא כְּעֵזֶר לְאָדָם,
דַּיֵּינוּ.

Ilu notsra Chava be'tselem Elohim
Velo ke'ezer le'Adam,
Dayenu.

If she had been created as Adam's equal
and not as temptress,
Dayenu.

אִילוּ נוֹצְרָה כְּשַׁוֶּוה לְאָדָם
וְלֹא כִּמְעוֹרֶרֶת יְצָרִים,
דַּיֵּנוּ.

Ilu notsra keshava le'Adam
Ve'lo keme'oreret yetsarim,
Dayenu.

If she were the first woman to eat
from the Tree of Knowledge,
who brought learning to us,
Dayenu.

אִילוּ הָיְתָה הָרִאשׁוֹנָה לִטְעוֹם מֵעֵץ הַדַּעַת
וְנָתְנָה לָנוּ אֶת הַלְּמִידָה,
דַּיֵּנוּ.

Ilu hayta harishona lit'om me'ets hada'at
Ve'natna lanu et halemida,
Dayenu.

If Sarah were recognized as a priestess,
royal in her own lineage,
Dayenu.

אִילוּ שָׂרָה הָיְתָה מוּכֶּרֶת כְּכֹהֶנֶת,
כְּמַלְכוּת בִּזְכוּת שׁוֹשַׁלְתָּה,
דַּיֵּנוּ.

Ilu Sarah hayta mukeret kekohenet,
Ke'malchut bizchut shoshalta,
Dayenu.

> *If Lot's wife had been pitied*
> *when she turned her head*
> *as the city swallowed her children,*
> *and not mocked with the falling,*
> *with the freezing of her tears,*
> *Dayenu.*

אִילוּ אֵשֶׁת לוֹט עוֹרְרָה רַחֲמִים
וְלֹא נִלְעֲגָה
כַּאֲשֶׁר הִפְנְתָה אֶת־רֹאשָׁהּ
בִּבְלֹעַ הָעִיר אֶת־יְלָדֶיהָ,
עַד שֶׁקָּפְאוּ דְּמָעוֹתֶיהָ,
דַּיֵּינוּ.

Ilu eshet Lot orera rachamim
Velo neel'aga
Ka'asher hifneta et rosha
Bivlo'a ha'ir et yeladey'ha,
Ad shekaf'u dim'otey'ha,
Dayenu.

> *If our foremothers had not been*
> > *considered*
> *as hardened roots*
> *or fruit-bearing wombs,*
> *but as women in themselves,*
> *Dayenu.*

אִילוּ לֹא חָשְׁבוּ אֶת אִימוֹתֵינוּ
כְּשׁוֹרָשִׁים עֲמוּקִים
אוֹ רַחֲמִים מֵנִבֵי פְּרִי,
אֶלָּא כְּנָשִׁים בִּזְכוּת עַצְמָן,
דַּיֵּנוּ.

Ilu lo chashvu et imoteinu
Keshorashim amukim
O rechamim meneevei pri,
Ela ke'nashim bizchut atsman,
Dayenu.

> If our fathers had not pitted our mothers
>   against each other,
> like Abraham with Sarah and Hagar
> or Jacob with Leah and Rachel
> or Elkanah with Hannah and Pnina,
> Dayenu.

אִילוּ לֹא שִׂיסוּ אֲבוֹתֵינוּ אֶת אִימוֹתֵינוּ
הָאַחַת בַּשְּׁנִייָה,
כְּמוֹ אַבְרָהָם אֶת שָׂרָה בְּהָגָר,
יַעֲקֹב אֶת לֵאָה בְּרָחֵל
אוֹ אֶלְקָנָה אֶת חַנָּה בִּפְנִנָּה,
דַּיֵּנוּ.

Ilu lo shissu avoteinu et imoteinu
Ha'achat bashneeya,
K'mo Avraham et Sarah be'Hagar
Ya'akov et Leah be'Rachel
O Elkana et Chana be'Fnina,
Dayenu.

If Miriam were given her prophet's chair
or the priesthood,
Dayenu.

אִילוּ קִיבְּלָה מִרְיָם אֶת כֵּס הַנְבוּאָה
אוֹ אֶת־הַכְּהוּנָה,
דַּיֵּינוּ.

Ilu kibla Miriam et kess ha'nevu'a
O et ha'kehuna,
Dayenu.

If the Just Women in Egypt
who caused our redemption
had been given sufficient recognition,
Dayenu.

אִילוּ צַדִּיקוֹת מִצְרַיִם
שֶׁהֵבִיאוּ לִגְאוּלַתֵינוּ
הָיוּ זוֹכוֹת הוֹקָרָה,
דַּיֵּינוּ.

Ilu tsadikot Mitzrayim
She'hevi'u lig'ulateinu
Hayu zochot hokara,
Dayenu.

If women bonding, like Naomi and
Ruth,
were the tradition
and not the exception,
Dayenu.

אִילוּ יַחְסֵי נָשִׁים, כְּמוֹ נָעֳמִי וְרוּת,
הָיוּ הַתָּדִיר
וְלֹא הַנָּדִיר,
דַּיֵּינוּ.

Ilu yachsey nashim, kmo Naomi ve'Rut,
Hayu ha'tadir
Ve'lo ha'nadir,
Dayenu.

If women had been in the Tribal
　　Council
and decided on the laws
that dealt with women,
Dayenu.

אִילוּ הָיוּ נָשִׁים בְּמוֹעֶצֶת הַשְּׁבָטִים
וְהֵן פָּסְקוּ אֶת־הַהֲלָכוֹת
שֶׁעִנְיָנָן בְּנָשִׁים,
דַּיֵּינוּ.

Ilu hayu nashim bemo'etset ha'shvatim
Vehen pasku et ha'halachot
She'inyanan benashim,
Dayenu.

If women had been
the writers of Tanach,
interpreters of our past,
Dayenu.

אִילוּ נָשִׁים
כָּתְבוּ אֶת הַמִּשְׁנָה
וּפִיעַנְחוּ אֶת עֲבָרֵינוּ,
דַּיֵּינוּ.

Ilu nashim
Katvu et ha'Mishna
U'fi'anchu et avareinu,
Dayenu.

If women had written the Haggadah
and brought our mothers forth,
Dayenu.

אִילוּ נָשִׁים כָּתְבוּ אֶת־הַהַגָּדָה
וְקִידְמוּ אֶת אִימוֹתֵינוּ,
דַּיֵּינוּ.

Ilu nashim katvu et ha'Haggadah
Ve'kidmu et imoteynu,
Dayenu.

If every generation of women
together with every generation of men
would continue to go out of Egypt,
Dayenu, Dayenu.

אִילוּ כֹּל דּוֹר וָדוֹר שֶׁל נָשִׁים
בְּצַוְותָא עִם כֹּל דּוֹר וָדוֹר שֶׁל גְּבָרִים
יַמְשִׁיכוּ בִּיצִיאַת מִצְרַיִם,
דַּיֵּינוּ, דַּיֵּינוּ.

Ilu kol dor va'dor shel nashim
Be'tsavta im kol dor va'dor shel gvarim
Yamshichu biytsi'at Mitzrayim,
Dayenu, Dayenu.

LO DAYENU

If the Shekhinah had brought us forth
from bondage
and had not educated us,
it would not have sufficed us.

אִילוּ הַשְׁכִינָה
שִׁחְרַרְתָנוּ מֵעַבְדוּת
וְלֹא חִינְכָה אוֹתָנוּ,
לֹא דַיֵינוּ.

Ilu ha'Shekhinah
Shichrartanu me'avdut
Ve'lo chincha otanu,
Lo Dayenu.

If She had educated us
and not given us opportunity to work,
it would not have sufficed us.

אִילוּ הַשְׁכִינָה חִינְכָה אוֹתָנוּ
וְלֹא נַתְנָה לָנוּ אֶפְשָׁרוּת לַעֲבוֹד,
לֹא דַיֵינוּ.

Ilu ha'Shekhinah chincha otanu,
Ve'lo natna lanu efsharut la'avod,
Lo Dayenu.

If She had given us opportunity to work
and not allowed us to advance,
it would not have sufficed us.

אִילוּ נָתְנָה לָנוּ הִזְדַמְנוּת לַעֲבוֹד
וְלֹא אִיפְשָׁרָה לָנוּ קִידוּם,
לֹא דַיֵינוּ.

Ilu natna lanu hizdamnut la'avod,
Ve'lo ifshera lanu kiddum,
Lo Dayenu.

If we were allowed to advance at work
but had to perform housewifely duties
as well,
Lo Dayenu.

אִילוּ הוּתַר לָנוּ קִידוּם בָּעֲבוֹדָה
וְעַדַיִין נִדְרַשְׁנוּ לַעֲסוֹק בְּעֲבוֹדוֹת הַבַּיִת,
לֹא דַיֵינוּ.

Ilu hutar lanu kiddum ba'avoda
Ve'adayin nidrashnu la'asok be'avodot habait,
Lo Dayenu.

If we were aided by rabbinical decree
and treated with dignity,
Dayenu, Dayenu. *It would suffice us.*

אִילוּ עָזְרוּ לָנוּ חוּקֵי הָרַבָּנִים
וְהִתְיַיחַסוּ אֵלֵינוּ בִּכְבוֹד,
דַּיֵּינוּ. דַּיֵּינוּ.

Ilu azru lanu chukei ha'rabanim
Ve'hityachasu eleinu be'chavod,
Dayenu. Dayenu.

"Did our mothers stay up all the night as we
here learning stay the night?" asked the Wise
Daughter.

SHE COULD NOT SLEEP THAT NIGHT

*When Sarah saw that she was barren
    and ill-regarded,
she could not sleep the decades of
    nights.*

*When Rebecca was taken from Aramea
to the strange land of Isaac,
she journeyed forth,
and did not sleep those nights.*

*When Leah was wed for only a week,
then had to share Jacob with her sister
    Rachel,*

she turned her face into the pillow
and did not sleep the night.

When Yocheved and Miriam planned
    the rescue,
they plaited reeds all the night,
and could not sleep that night.

When Ziporah the Midianite
was left behind with her two sons
while Moses went back into Egypt,
she could not sleep the nights.

When Miriam celebrated the
    Redemption,
she gathered the women,
and they danced and sang all the night.
They could not sleep that night.

When Miriam was cast low,
she paced her tent in anger,
and could not sleep the night.

When Deborah, the judge,
marched with the army to war,
she could not sleep the embattled
    nights.

When Yael, from the house of Ziporah,
murdered General Sisera,
she had not slept that night.

When Judith prayed from dusk to dawn
planning against Holofernes,
she did not sleep all that night.

When women plan their lives,
their battles and escapes,
they do not sleep the night.

We here gathered learning
on the Night of Vigil
will not easily sleep this night.

"I am tired of Miriam," says the Wicked Daughter. "When will you find her?"

The One Who Does Not Know How to Question looks at the Mothers.
The Mothers answer the unasked question:

F O L L O W I N G   M I R I A M

We follow her cape,
through the cold night air.
We follow her wrapped figure
under the hot sun
to places unknown.
We entreat her to halt, to recognize us.
What is the way? we ask.
Her footsteps disappear
in the sand.
We find the map as we go along.

Lift the fourth cup.

THIS IS THE FOURTH CUP OF WINE.

We drink the fourth cup of wine, saying:
"I have been in Egypt. I have been in the desert.
I have learned our history. And I am still on my
journey."

גַּרְתִּי בְּמִצְרַיִם. שָׁכַנְתִּי בַּמִּדְבָּר.
לָמַדְתִּי אֶת עֲבָרֵנוּ. וְאֲנִי עֲדַיִין בְּדַרְכִּי.

Garti be'Mitzrayim. Shachanti ba'midbar.
Lamadeti et a'varenu. Ve'ani adayin bedarcki.

We have ended the Passover service
according to its order and new customs.

Under the wings of the Shekhinah, we fly
homeward to Zion in song.

"The Women's Seder is ended?" asks the
Simple Daughter.
"Soon," say the Mothers. "Someone is
waiting for us."
The Mothers and Daughters open the door.

Miriam ha Neviah
Miriam from the House of Levy
Soon will come to us
with timbel and song
Miriam, our prophet,
will dance with us.

הַנְבִיאַה מִרְיָם
מִרְיָם מִבֵּית לֵוִי
בִּמְהֵירָה תָבוֹא אֵלֵינוּ
בְּתוּפִּים וּבְזִימְרָה
מִרְיָם, נְבִיאַתֵנוּ
תֵרַקֵד עִימָנוּ.

Ha'Neviah'a Miriam
Miriam me'beit Levi
Bim'heira tavo eleinu
Be'tupim u'be'zimra
Miriam, ne'vi'atenu
Teraked imanu.

Miriam enters for the Festival Meal.